HOW TO HANDLE YOUR EMOTIONS

A must know tips on how to handle your emotions (master your emotion)

James Kessler

Table of contents

Chapter 1

Meaning of Emotion

Emotions are mental states triggered by neurophysiological adjustments; they are differently linked to ideas, sensations, behavioral reactions, and a level of pleasure or discomfort. Emotions and mood, temperament, personality, disposition, and creativity are frequently linked.

Emotions cause various physiological, behavioral, and cognitive changes. From a mechanistic perspective, emotions may be described as "a happy or negative sensation that is coupled with a specific pattern of physiological activity."

Emotions' initial purpose was to elicit adaptive responses that, in the past, would have aided in the kin selection, reproduction, and transmission of genes through survival.

According to certain ideas, emotion has a significant cognitive component. However, according to certain ideas, emotion may exist independently of and even come before knowledge. Consciously feeling an emotion is displaying a mental image of that emotion from a real or imagined event that is connected to a positive or negative internal state.
The verbal descriptions of experiences that describe an internal state serve to establish the content states.

Emotions are intricate. On the subject of whether or not emotions alter our behavior, there are several theories. On the one hand, autonomic nervous arousal and the physiology of feeling are strongly related. Behavior propensity and emotion are related.

People who are extroverts are more prone to interact with others and express their feelings than introverts.

People are more inclined to hide their feelings and become more socially aloof. Motivation is frequently fueled by emotion.

On the other hand, emotions are only syndromes of components rather than actual causes. These components may include motivation, mood, behavior, and physiological changes, but none of these constitutes emotion. Additionally, none of these elements are caused by emotion.

Subjective experience, cognitive processes, expressive behavior, psychophysiological changes, and instrumental conduct are only a few of the components that make up emotions. Academics formerly made an effort to link emotion to one of its constituent parts, such as a subjective experience, instrumental action, physiological changes, and so forth. More recently, it has been asserted that emotion consists of all the elements.

Depending on the academic field, the various elements of emotion are classified somewhat differently. Emotion is often defined as a subjective, aware experience that is largely manifested through psychophysiological manifestations, biological responses, and mental states in psychology and philosophy.

Sociology uses a similar multi-component model of emotion. Peggy Thoits, for instance, defined emotions as including physical characteristics, cultural or emotional labels (anger, surprise, etc.), expressive bodily movements, and the evaluation of circumstances and surroundings.

There are certain emotional links and direct opposites, and emotions have been classified. Graham classifies emotions as either functioning or dysfunctional, and he claims that all functioning emotions have advantages.

Emotions can refer to strong feelings that are directed against someone or something in specific contexts. On the other hand, minor emotions (such as being irritated or content) and undirected emotions can also be referred to as emotions (as in anxiety and depression).

One area of study examines how the word "emotion" is used in common speech and discovers that this usage differs significantly from that in scholarly discourse.

Maxim Deras described emotions as the outcome of a cognitive and conscious process that takes place in response to a physical system's reaction to a trigger.

Chapter 2

How your environment affect your emotion

If you think that your environment and your emotions are two entirely separate things — think again! It turns out that there are profound and intimate links between them, and one is not always separable from the other. Living in a dirty, messy home, for instance, is damaging to mental health. It creates chaos and clutter when your unconscious mind wants to order and stability. The type of city you live in also makes a difference. People who live in polluted or dangerous areas tend to have lower wellness scores than those that live in happy, productive, and clean locations.

Multiple environmental factors play into your mental health. However, as you might expect, each person is different — what affects one person might not affect another. Here's how environmental factors impact your mental health, and what you can do about them.

Your environment impacts your well being

Researchers claim that a variety of environmental variables affect how you feel. These include the actual surroundings as well as the sense of community. For instance, the place in which you live might have an impact. When people live in lovely, snug, and warm homes, their levels of well-being tend to be greater. Their dwellings serve as a sort of "recharge station," allowing them to face the difficulties of the outside world with more assurance. When houses are neglected, filthy, or moist, well-being tends to suffer.

Another element is your community. Independent of the impacts of the crime itself, places with greater crime rates often have lower levels of well-being.

The ramifications it has on our mental health are intriguing regarding this. The majority of adult life is spent at work, at home, or in other artificial settings. Moving from one area to another can have a significant impact on a person's mood. Some depressed persons discover that spending time in nature helps to reduce their symptoms.

Additionally, social contexts have a significant role. Lack of support makes people more likely to have mental health issues. When others are there, it is simpler to deal with. People who have friends, family, roommates, and a sense of community tend to handle pressures more readily than those who don't.

There is some evidence that your mood may be impacted by lighting conditions. Living in well-lit regions often makes people feel better than in gloomy, dark places. There isn't enough light in cellars for individuals to keep their body clocks in sync, which is one of the reasons many people choose not to live there.

Your Mental Health and Environmental Factors

Here are a few of the particular elements that have an impact on how you see and interpret your surroundings. These effects all elicit various psychological reactions.

Familiarity

Your feelings towards a place might change depending on how familiar you are with it. You will truly feel this in your body when you get home if you have favorable associations with coming to your parents' place. You can get a sense of tranquility or peace that you just can't get anywhere else.

The situation can, however, also be reversed. When it brings back painful memories from the past or serves as a reminder of unpleasant experiences, familiarity can be a bad thing.

By changing the surroundings, you may modify the familiarity level in your house. Consider hanging familiar items, such as souvenirs or pictures of your family, from the walls or above the fireplace. These may quietly alter your state of mind and increase your sense of place.

Likewise, if these things are upsetting you, you might also wish to remove them.

People

Spending time with certain people might have a big influence on how you feel. You'll believe that you can do almost whatever you desire in life if you surround yourself with inspiring individuals who encourage you. Life will also seem like a never-ending sequence of struggles if you surround yourself with negative people who drag you down.

So be cautious about who you let into your spaces. Your mental health is supported by interactions with less conflict and kindness. Accept their tranquility, even if it doesn't always feel thrilling.

Senses

Your mood may also be significantly impacted by an environment's colors, scents, and lighting. Shutter manufacturers are fully aware of this. They are aware that how people feel in a space is influenced by the amount of light that enters there. Your normal sleep-wake cycle can be adjusted when light levels are high, as they should be throughout the day.

Unwanted sounds might cause issues. So that sirens, traffic noises, and even the weather don't disrupt their peace of mind, a lot of individuals build sound insulation.

Cleanliness

Your degree of cleanliness can significantly affect how you feel. Your subconscious is affected by the cleanliness of your rooms. Your ability to relax in life and have less to worry about depends on how uncluttered your environment is.

If you must surround yourself with items, make sure they have significance. Don't overcrowd your house with items that don't genuinely enhance the experience of living there.

Culture

To prevent feeling more deeply alone, it is essential to contact individuals who have similar cultures and beliefs to you. It might be isolating to have beliefs that other people don't share. Perhaps your political views or culinary preferences differ from those of the people around you, or you are looking for a different sort of spiritual experience.

You need to find others who share your views in this case. You'll want people you can relate to, who share your interests and outlook on life.

Focus on the Things You Can Control

It could first feel a little intimidating to change your environment. After all, certain circumstances are beyond your control. You cannot, for example.
Reduce the amount of crime in your neighborhood. The police and lawmakers should handle that.

Here, the key is to concentrate only on your controllable actions.

Consider making changes in the areas of your life that will most affect how you feel

For instance, organizing your bedroom is a wonderful place to start. You want a spot you can go to at night that will help you unwind and get a good night's sleep. The kitchen may be the next stop. When there is a mound of dirty dishes in the sink, it is never fun to prepare a meal from scratch.

Adapt your connections

Spend time with uplifting individuals that will raise you and assist you in achieving your personal goals. Avoid those who make you feel exhausted or are abusive in any way. Be very selective about the friends you choose.

Change how you see things

You may also try changing the way you see things. Your mental health is significantly impacted by the way you choose to view the world. You'll always feel uneasy if you think the danger is lurking around every turn. However, you will succeed if you seize opportunities and don't take yourself too seriously. When you sometimes lower the dial, things get simpler.

Developing a routine might be beneficial. You get a sense of control when you have routines, which gives you the freedom to go after the things in life you truly desire.

Chapter 3

Understanding your emotion

What are you feeling, right now, as you start to read this? Are you curious? Hopeful that you'll learn something about yourself? Bored because this is something you have to do for school and you're not really into it — or happy because it's a school project you enjoy? Perhaps you're distracted by something else, like feeling excited about your weekend plans or sad because you just went through a breakup.

Emotions like these are part of human nature. They give us information about what we're experiencing and help us know how to react.

We sense our emotions from the time we're babies. Infants and young children react to their emotions with facial expressions or with actions like laughing, cuddling, or crying. They feel and show emotions, but they can't yet name the emotion or say why they feel that way.

As we grow up, we become more skilled in understanding emotions. Instead of just reacting as little kids do, we can identify what we feel and put it into words. With time and practice, we get better at knowing what we are feeling and why. This skill is called emotional awareness.

Emotional awareness helps us know what we need and want (or don't want!). It helps us build better relationships. That's because being aware of our emotions can help us talk about feelings more clearly, avoid or resolve conflicts better, and move past difficult feelings more easily.

Some people are naturally more in touch with their emotions than others. The good news is, that everyone can be more aware of their emotions. It just takes practice. But it's worth the effort: Emotional awareness is the first step toward building emotional intelligence, a skill that can help people succeed in life.

Here are a few basic things about emotions:

Emotions come and go: Most of us feel many different emotions throughout the day. Some last just a few seconds. Others might linger to become a mood.
Emotions can be mild, intense, or anywhere in between. The intensity of an emotion can depend on the situation and the person.

There are no good or bad emotions, but there are good and bad ways of expressing (or acting on) emotions. Learning how to express emotions in acceptable ways is a separate skill — managing emotions — that is built on a foundation of being able to understand emotions.
It's All Good

Some emotions feel positive — like feeling happy, loving, confident, inspired, cheerful, interested, grateful, or included. Other emotions can seem more negative — like feeling angry,
resentful, afraid, ashamed, guilty, sad, or worried. Both positive and negative emotions are normal.

All emotions tell us something about ourselves and our situation. But sometimes we find it hard to accept what we feel. We might judge ourselves for feeling a certain way, like if we feel jealous, for example. But instead of thinking we shouldn't feel that way, it's better to notice how we feel.

Avoiding negative feelings or pretending we don't feel the way we do can backfire. It's harder to move past difficult feelings and allow them to fade if we don't face them and try to understand why we feel that way.

You don't have to dwell on your emotions or constantly talk about how you feel. Emotional awareness simply means recognizing, respecting, and accepting your feelings as they happen.

Building Emotional Awareness

Emotional awareness helps us know and accept ourselves. So how can you become more aware of your emotions? Start with these three simple steps:

Make a habit of tuning in to how you feel in different situations throughout the day. You might notice that you feel excited after making plans to go somewhere with a friend. Or that you feel nervous before an exam.

You might be relaxed when listening to music, inspired by an art exhibit, or pleased when a friend compliments you. Simply notice whatever emotion you feel, then name that emotion in your mind.

It only takes a second to do this, but it's great practice. Notice that each emotion passes and makes room for the next experience.

Rate how strong the feeling is. After you notice and name an emotion, take it a step further: Rate how strongly you feel the emotion on a scale of 1–10, with 1 being the mildest feeling and 10 being the most intense.

Share your feelings with the people closest to you. This is the best way to practice putting emotions into words, a skill that helps us feel closer to friends, boyfriends or girlfriends, parents, coaches — anyone.

Make it a daily practice to share feelings with a friend or family member. You could share something quite personal or something that's simply an everyday emotion.

Just like anything else in life, when it comes to emotions, practice makes perfect! Remind yourself there are no good or bad emotions. Don't judge your feelings – just keep noticing and naming them.

Before you read on, take a moment to pause. Close your eyes if you want to, and take a couple of calm breaths. Then ask yourself – how are you feeling right now?
Think of one-word answers that describe how you feel.

Notice what words come to mind. Does one feel stand out? Or are there a few? You might even have opposite feelings at the same time. For example, excited and nervous. That's normal.

Just notice the emotions you feel at the moment. There's no right or wrong answer.

Doing this is a simple way to be aware of your emotions.

Sometimes it's easy to be aware of your emotions. Maybe there's one feeling that's strong and obvious to you. Other times, you might not pay much attention to how you feel. But your emotions are there. And they're all normal.

Feelings are signals from the body that help us understand ourselves and make good decisions. For example, feeling fear in a situation like crossing the street in traffic is a useful signal to stay safe.

Being more aware of your emotions is a skill that can help you:

know yourself better
feel better about things and cope better

be less self-critical
pause instead of acting on difficult emotions
decide how to act and handle situations
get along better with others

Here are five ways to practice being more aware of your emotions:

Notice and name your feelings: To start, just notice how you feel as things happen. Say the name of the feeling to yourself. You might feel proud when something goes well.

Or disappointed if you don't do well on a test. You might feel relaxed when sitting with friends at lunch. Or nervous before a test.

Track one emotion: Pick one emotion — like feeling glad. Track it all day. Notice how often you feel it. Maybe you're glad when something good happens. Or glad when a friend shows up.

Maybe you're glad when someone lends you a hand or says a kind word. Or glad just because it's Friday. Every time you feel glad, make a mental note to yourself or write it down. Is the feeling mild, medium, or strong?

Learn new words for feelings: How many feeling words can you name? Try to think of even more. How many words are there for anger? For example, you might be annoyed, upset, or mad. You might be irate, fuming, or outraged.

Keep a feelings journal: Take a few minutes each day to write about how you feel and why. Writing about your feelings helps you get to know them better.

Make art, write poetry, or compose music to express an emotion you feel.

Notice feelings in art, songs, and movies. Focus on what the artist did to show those feelings. How do you feel in response?

Take time to get to know your emotions better. Just notice how you feel. Accept how you feel without judging yourself. Show yourself some kindness.

Remind yourself that all your emotions are normal. But how you act on emotions matters a lot. When you know your emotions, you're better able to make wise choices about how to act — no matter what you're feeling.

If you have emotions that feel difficult or overwhelming, get support. An adult you trust can help you talk through any tough feelings you're dealing with. Sometimes people get help from a therapist to deal with difficult emotions that affect daily life.

How to Correct your emotion

You might be surprised to learn how vital it is to have the capacity to feel and express emotions.

Emotions are a major factor in your reactions since they represent your emotional response to a circumstance. When you're tuned in to them, you have access to crucial information that supports:

Decision-making
relationships that work
regular encounters
Self-care

While emotions can be beneficial in daily life, when they feel out of control, they can hurt your emotional well-being and interpersonal connections.

Any feeling, including those you may consider pleasant, like elation or delight, can get so strong that it becomes hard to regulate.

You can regain control, though, with a little work. According to two research from 2010Trusted Source, emotional control abilities are related to wellbeing. Additionally, the second study discovered a probable connection between these abilities and financial success, so investing some time in that area may pay dividends.

To get you started, consider the following advice.

1. Examine the effect of your feelings.
Not all strong emotions are negative.

According to Botnick, emotions give our life excitement, individuality, and vibrancy. Strong emotions may indicate that we completely embrace life and aren't suppressing our innate responses.

It's very normal to occasionally feel emotionally overwhelmed—whether something beautiful or dreadful occurs when you feel like you've missed out, occurs.

So, how can you recognize an issue when it arises?

Frequently irrational emotions can result in:

Conflict in a friendship or relationship
a problem connecting with people
complications at job or school
an impulse to take drugs to assist control your emotions

emotional or physical outbursts

Take some time to evaluate how your irrational emotions are impacting your daily life. This will make it easy to identify problem areas (and measure your success) (and track your success).

2. Instead of repression, aim for regulation.

If it were that simple to regulate your emotions, you could do it with a dial. But consider for a second that you could control your emotions in this manner.

You wouldn't want to leave them operating at full capacity constantly. You wouldn't want to completely turn them off either.

You restrict yourself from feeling and expressing emotions when you suppress or repress them. This may occur intentionally (suppression) or unintentionally (repression).

Both can lead to signs of physical and mental illness, such as:

Anxiety
Depression
sleep problems

muscle spasms and discomfort
Stress management issues
abuse of substances

Make sure you aren't just brushing your emotions under the rug while you are trying to regulate them. It's important to strike a balance between having too many feelings and having none at all for healthy emotional expression.

How to evolve while feeling emotion

3. Determine your feelings.

You may start taking back control by taking a moment to check in with your emotions.

Let's say you've been dating someone for a while. You attempted to set up a date with them last week, but they declined. You contacted me once more yesterday with the message, "I'd want to meet you soon. Can we get together this week? ”

After more than a day, they finally respond: "Can't. Busy."

All of a sudden, you're quite upset. You fling your phone across the room, tip your trash can over, and kick your desk, stabbing your toe, all without pausing to think.

Stop yourself and inquire:

What am I now feeling? (disappointed, perplexed, and enraged)
What took occurred to give me this feeling? (They dismissed me with a no).

Exists an alternate explanation for the circumstance that would make sense? (They could intend to provide more details when they can; they could be under stress, ill, or dealing with something else they don't feel comfortable disclosing.)
What do I want to do in response to these emotions? (Scream, toss things in anger, and send an offensive text back.)

Is there a more effective method of handling them? (Ask if everything is well; inquire as to when they will be free next; go for a run or stroll.)
You can change your first, extreme response by reframing your thinking to take into account potential alternatives.

It could take some time before this reaction gets ingrained in you. Practice will make it simpler to mentally do these actions (and more effective).

4. Accept all of your feelings.

Try downplaying your feelings to yourself if you want to improve your ability to control your emotions.

It may seem beneficial to tell yourself, "Just calm down," or "It's not that big of an issue, so don't stress out," when you start to hyperventilate after hearing wonderful news or collapse on the floor weeping and shouting when you can't locate your keys.

However, this discredits your experience. To you, it is really important.

You can become more at ease with your emotions if you accept them as they are. You may feel powerful emotions more thoroughly and avoid excessive, counterproductive reactions by increasing your comfort level with them.

Regulate
Name that
Take them in
Journal
Breathe
Read the room
Get some space
Meditate
Reduce stress

Exists an alternate explanation for the circumstance that would make sense? (Perhaps they're under stress, ill, or coping with another issue that they don't feel comfortable disclosing. They could want to provide further details when they can.)
What do I want to do in response to these emotions? (Scream, toss things in anger, and send an offensive text back.)

5. Maintain a mood diary

Your sentiments and the reactions they elicit can be written down (or typed out), which can help you identify any problematic tendencies.

Sometimes it's sufficient to mentally follow your thoughts back via your emotions. Writing down emotions might help you think about them more thoroughly.

It also aids in identifying the situations that lead to emotions that are more difficult to manage, such as difficulties at work or family conflicts.

Finding precise triggers enables the development of more effective management techniques.

When you journal every day, it is extremely beneficial. Keep a diary close by and record strong feelings or emotions as they arise. Try to keep track of your reaction and the triggers. If your response wasn't helpful, utilize your diary to research further potential solutions that could.

Emotions are a major factor in your reactions since they represent your emotional response to a circumstance. When you're tuned in to them, you have access to crucial information that supports:

Making decisions Relationship success

regular encounters
Self-care

While emotions might be beneficial in your day-to-day existence, When they feel out of control, they can hurt your emotional well-being and interpersonal connections.

Any feeling, including those you may consider pleasant, like happiness or delight, can amplify to the point that it becomes hard to regulate.

You can regain control, though, with a little work. According to two research from 2010Trusted Source, emotional control abilities are related to wellbeing. Additionally, the second study discovered a probable connection between these abilities and financial success, so investing some time in that area may pay dividends.

6. Inhale deeply.

Whether you're exuberantly joyful or furiously upset and unable to speak, there is much to be said about the power of taking a deep breath.
Even if that's not the intention, slowing down and focusing on your breathing won't make the feelings go away.

However, practicing deep breathing can help you center yourself, and take a step back from the initial, overwhelming emotion, and any excessive reaction you'd want to avoid.

When your emotions start to overtake you in the future:

Inhale gently. The diaphragm, not the chest, is where deep breaths originate. Visualizing your breath rising from your abdomen may be of assistance.
Retain it. Breathe in for three counts, then gently let it out.

Think of a mantra. Repetition of a mantra, such as "I am peaceful" or "I am relaxed," might be useful for certain people.

7. Recognize when to use your voice

Everything has its own time and place, including strong emotions. For instance, crying uncontrollably after losing a loved one is a very typical reaction. After getting dumped, screaming or even beating your pillow may help you release some tension and fury.

However, in other circumstances, some restraint is required. No matter how angry you are about an unfair disciplinary action, yelling at your supervisor won't solve the problem.

You may learn when it's OK to express your sentiments and when you might want to sit with them for the time being by being aware of your surroundings and the scenario.

8. Make room for yourself

According to Botnick, separating yourself from strong emotions might help you ensure that you're responding to them rationally.

Physical separation, such as leaving a distressing circumstance, might constitute this distance. But by diverting your attention, you may also establish some mental space.

It's not healthy to completely ignore or avoid feelings, but it's also okay to divert your attention from them until you're in a better position to deal with them. Just be sure to visit them again. Healthy diversion only lasts for a short time.

Try:

going for a stroll
viewing a humorous video

conversing with a loved one
Having a brief conversation with your pet

9. Attempt meditation.

If you already meditate, it could be one of your go-to strategies for handling strong emotions.

You may become more conscious of all emotions and sensations by practicing meditation. By meditating, you're training yourself to sit with those emotions and recognize them without criticizing or trying to modify or suppress them.

Emotional control may be made simpler by learning to accept all of your feelings, as was already indicated. You may improve these accepting abilities by meditating. Other advantages include improving your ability to unwind and sleep better.

10. Manage your stress well

It might be challenging to control your emotions when you're under a lot of stress. Even those who typically have good emotional self-control may find it more difficult to do so in conditions of extreme stress and anxiety.

Your emotions can become more controllable by reducing stress or learning more effective stress management techniques.

Meditation and other mindfulness techniques can reduce stress as well. They won't eliminate it, but they can make it more bearable.

Other beneficial techniques for managing stress include:

obtaining adequate sleep, having time for friends to visit and laugh, exercising spending time in the outdoors, and creating time for leisure activities

11. Consult a counselor

If your feelings are still too much for you to handle, it might be time to get some professional help.

Several mental health illnesses, including bipolar disorder and borderline personality disorder, are associated with long-term or persistent emotional dysregulation and mood swings. According to Botnick, having trouble managing your emotions might also be related to trauma, familial problems, or other underlying difficulties.

A therapist may provide you with sympathetic, nonjudgmental assistance as you:

investigate the causes of poorly controlled emotions

Mood swings and intense emotions can result in negative or unwanted thoughts that eventually result in feelings of hopelessness or despair. Addressing severe mood swings can teach you how to down-regulate intense feelings or up-regulate limited emotional expression. Practice challenging and reframing feelings that cause distress.

This loop may eventually result in unproductive coping mechanisms like self-harm or even suicidal thoughts. Speak to a loved one you can trust if you start to experience suicidal thoughts or desire to hurt yourself so they can assist you and receive support immediately away.

Chapter 4

How to grow with your emotion

Success has many facets, and having money is simply one of them. Success, however, also entails a sense of well-being, vigor, and excitement for life, satisfying relationships, creative freedom, emotional and psychological stability, and peace of mind. — Deepak Chopra

I frequently hear success tales involving money. But despite how much I appreciate them, there are times when I wish I could hear more emotional triumph stories. Do we have the ability to achieve both financial and emotional success at the same time, or are they incompatible?

Everyone enjoys hearing about how someone overcomes adversity to climb the financial ladder of success. We adore them, even more, when they were raised in difficult conditions and endured abuse, neglect, and bullying in addition to growing up without access to adequate resources.

We feel like we can join them in their joy when they finally figure out how to succeed in one area of their lives. But whenever I hear these success tales, I can't help but wonder: Does the monetary stability and contentment that come with achieving childhood professional ambitions make everything better?

Does all the emotional suffering just go away when someone reaches the pinnacle of success by being a well-known movie director, CEO, physician, partner at a law firm, or professional athlete?

We look up to persons who are successful in their jobs because we believe they have had everything and have permanently overcome the hopelessness of their youth. However, if we take a deeper look, we can discover that material success and emotional achievement aren't always synonymous.

When we achieve our professional aspirations, we frequently assume that the issues that may have initially motivated us to succeed won't trouble us anymore. I don't believe that material and emotional success are synonymous, though.

I prefer to hear about successful individuals, who have a full emotional life filled with personal fulfillment and manage to remain composed in the face of adversity. Having relationships and a strong sense of self.

Even if it seems corny, if I had to pick, I would rather be emotionally stable than lonely and alone inside my beachside home. However, perhaps we are not forced to pick between the two. Maybe we can smile with our friends and family, look out over the beach, sip pricey champagne, and be emotionally and financially happy.

My fundamental argument is that, as a society, we think that achieving our professional objectives would lead to happiness, freedom from stress and problems, and freedom from the past. However, there are innumerable instances of successful individuals who have ruined their personal life, interpersonal connections, and families. Their loneliness, anxiety, drug use, anger management difficulties, flashbacks, etc. were not resolved by their financial success. None of them were able to improve their ability to control their emotions or their most trying relationships as a result.

I view emotional maturity as the ability to successfully manage life while having a strong sense of self, agency, and competence. All of this may be done along the route to financial success or before it. Even if we accomplish all of our professional and financial objectives, we won't necessarily be emotionally successful.

Let me describe the characteristics of an emotionally successful person in more detail. The fact that they are grown individuals who recognize that despite all the positive things in life, there are sometimes difficult moments does not hinder or hold them back. These people are typically content with their lives, themselves, and their choices.

When someone behaves badly or says something hurtful, they don't let it break them or spoil their day. They have strong, mutually satisfying friendships and familial ties.

They prefer engaging in constructive activities to negative ones. They efficiently control their negative emotions as they arise, allowing them to carry on with their everyday activities while feeling down. They recognize that their value originates from inside, not from other people, things, or events outside of themselves, and they don't place responsibility for their problems on others. Overall, they make good companions, work well in partnerships, are adept at controlling their emotions, and accept personal responsibility. Being emotionally successful sounds wonderful, right?

what is emotional success? Well, some individuals seek help from therapists, life coaches, yoga instructors, meditators, workshops, seminars, or self-help books. Each new piece of knowledge advances us, enabling us to comprehend both our behaviors and those of others.

We inherited particular methods of handling problems and controlling our emotions under particular conditions depending on our families of origin. In essence, our families deal each of us a certain hand, and it is up to us to decide how to play it.

There is a means to alter our cards if we are unhappy with them and to focus on improving ourselves so that we, too, can behave in ways that are more consistent with our beliefs and objectives and be emotionally successful.

The strategies listed below can assist you in achieving emotional success.

1. Develop Objectivity - It's critical to become impartial when assessing your emotional process. We all respond to circumstances automatically, as I already indicated, because of the influences of our families of origin. Instead of instinctively responding to circumstances, it is preferable to develop objectivity through learning to examine your behavior. Keep in mind that your difficulties today are not a result of the past; rather, they are a result of how you are

resolving a problem today, which may have been influenced by the past. Successful emotional persons develop self-awareness and objectivity regarding their emotional processes so they may make better decisions regarding how to react to their present circumstances.

2. Develop a Strong Sense of Self - Having a strong sense of self will make you less anxious, less prone to reacting to others' expectations, and less dependent on the approval or attention of others. It all comes down to learning how to express yourself, bringing self-awareness to your network of interactions, and developing autonomy within those networks.

sometimes you'll feel bad in your life. Knowing how to best soothe yourself when the pain comes is the best way to handle it.

Soothing yourself includes self-regulating and managing your emotions on your own, without needing other people or things (like alcohol, food, shopping, etc.) to calm you down. When you're able to self-regulate, you don't adjust your internal functioning for others and, instead, can focus on yourself and your needs.

3. Learn to Adapt to Change - How effectively a person can adapt to change affects how they react to the people and situations in their lives. Adaptation difficulties are reflected in psychological or physical symptoms.

Even under pressure, emotionally successful people can maintain positive relationships with others. They allocate their life force in useful ways to make efficient use of it. They practice controlling their ingrained, innate stress reactions, such as the want to shout, retreat, drink, gamble, or act violently.

Those who are adaptable can overcome adversity by reflecting on their actions and reactions.

4. Develop Self-Regulation - Being emotionally successful requires you to master this skill. There is no avoiding it:

5. Establish Boundaries - Knowing who you are, how you feel, and what you like and hate are all important aspects of this. When the people in your life respect your boundaries and you have healthy relationships that balance giving and receiving, you are emotionally successful.
The emotionally successful individual can effectively convey when a boundary has been breached.

Grow Yourself Up - By this, I mean developing the ability to examine yourself in the context of your interactions and realizing that issues arise more from connections than from people. When we can be more honest with ourselves and with how we interact with others—not because we're at fault, but we can declare that we've developed because we understand that we're accountable for our actions.

7. Control Your Anxiety - Anxiety makes things that don't exist. It is a major source of emotions and can make our lives extremely anxious. We all experience fear, thus it's acceptable to feel it. Your amount of emotional success is determined by how you deal with your fear.

8. Create a Strong Internal Sense of Self-Worth - A strong internal sense of self-worth is crucial for emotional achievement. When you are emotionally successful, you validate your value rather than other people, things, or outside events.

Emotionally successful people are aware of their special calling. They refuse to accept the message that they are unworthy of their environment or from other people. Your level of security will increase organically once you realize that you're perfect just the way you are.

There are many strategies to increase emotional success and maturity, but the majority of the key changes to develop take place in our important interactions. I used to believe that my primary objectives were to succeed professionally and become financially secure.

I'm not suggesting those things aren't significant; nevertheless, focusing just on those two constricted my perspective and led to a significant blind spot in my life. To be fulfilled in our lives and relationships, it is more crucial than ever to become conscious of our emotional maturity.

We are at a moment where we have limitless opportunities to develop and can become who we want to be without suffering significant consequences. We must always keep in mind that we are in complete control of our life, making the effort to develop emotional independence an invaluable objective.

What, in your opinion, qualifies a person as emotionally successful or mature? What has aided your personal development and maturation? I'm interested in hearing your opinions.

Chapter 5

50 tips for improving your emotional intelligence

Emotional intelligence fuels your performance both in the workplace and in your personal life, but it starts with you. From your confidence, empathy, and optimism to your social skills and self-control, understanding and managing your own emotions can accelerate success in all areas of your life.

No matter what professional field you are in, whether you manage a team of two or 20, or even just yourself, realizing how effective you are at controlling your emotional energy is a great starting point. Absent from the curriculum, emotional intelligence isn't something we are taught or tested on, so where did it come from, what is it, do you have it, and is it that important?

Fortunately, it is something you can learn and we've compiled a comprehensive list of tips to help you explore your level of emotional intelligence and gain important emotional intelligence skills that can be implemented into everyday life. Some of these tips we follow ourselves and others have been revealed to us by our amazing clients and partners who know how to motivate and inspire their teams but first and foremost, themselves.

Skip to a specific section?

1. Emotional Intelligence
2. Self-awareness
3. Self-management
4. Motivation
5. Empathy
6. Social skills
7. What to avoid

EMOTIONAL INTELLIGENCE

Put simply, emotional Intelligence is how well individuals identify and manage their own emotions and react to the emotions of others. It's understanding how those emotions shape your thoughts and actions so you can have greater control over your behavior and develop the skills to manage yourself more effectively. Becoming more emotionally conscious allows us to grow and gain a deeper understanding of who we are, enabling us to communicate better with others and build stronger relationships.

We suggest starting with these initial 8 tips, they provide a good starting point to Discovering the foundations of your emotional intelligence.

1) Practice observing how you feel

Often we lead hectic, busy lifestyles and it's all too easy for us to lose touch with our emotions. To reconnect, try setting a timer for various points during the day. When the timer goes off, take a few deep breaths and notice how you're feeling emotionally. Pay attention to where that emotion is showing up as a physical feeling in your body and what the sensation feels like. The more you practice, the more it will become second nature.

2) Pay attention to how you behave

While you're practicing your emotional awareness, take the time to notice your behavior too. Observe how you act when you're experiencing certain emotions, and how that affects your day-to-day life. Managing our emotions becomes easier once we become more conscious of how we react to them.

3) Question your own opinions

In this hyper-connected world, it is easy to fall into an 'opinion bubble'. This is a state of existence where your own opinions are constantly reinforced by people with similar viewpoints. Take time to read the other side of the story and have your views challenged (even if you still feel they are right). This will help you understand other people and be more receptive to new ideas.

4) Take responsibility for your feelings

Your emotions and behavior come from you, they don't come from anyone else, and once you start accepting responsibility for how you feel and how you behave it will have a positive impact on all areas of your life.

5) Take time to celebrate the positive

A key part of emotional intelligence is celebrating and reflecting on the positive moments in life. People who experience positive emotions are generally more resilient and more likely to have fulfilling relationships, which will help them move past adversity.

6) But don't ignore the negative

Reflecting on negative feelings is just as important as reflecting on the positive. Understanding why you feel negative is key to becoming a fully-rounded individual, who is more able to deal with negative issues in the future.

7) Don't forget to breathe

Life throws various situations our way, with most of us experiencing some sort of stress regularly. To manage your emotions when this happens and to avoid outbursts, don't forget to breathe. Call a time out and go put some cold water on your face, go outside and get some fresh air or make a drink – anything to keep your cool and give yourself a chance to get a hold on what's happening and how you should respond.

8) A lifetime process

Understand and remember that emotional intelligence is something you develop and requires continual improvement; it's very much a lifetime practice.

SELF AWARENESS

A key component of emotional intelligence, self-awareness is the ability to recognize and understand your character, moods, and emotions and their effect on others. It includes a realistic self-assessment of what you're capable of – your strengths and weaknesses – and knowing how others perceive you. It can help highlight areas for self-improvement, make you better at adapting, and can limit wrongful decisions.

9) Learn to look at yourself objectively

Knowing yourself completely is difficult and it's almost impossible to look at yourself objectively, so input from those who know you is vital. Ask them where your strengths and weaknesses lie, write down what they say, and compare them. Look out for any patterns and remember not to argue with them – it doesn't mean they're right – they're just trying to help you gauge your perception from another's point of view.

10) Keep a diary

A great way to get an accurate gauge of yourself is to keep a diary. Start by writing down what happened to you at the end of every day, how it made you feel, and how you dealt with it. Documenting details like these will make you more aware of what you're doing and will highlight where problems might be coming from. Periodically, look back over your comments and take note of any trends.

11) Understand what motivates you

Everyone has a core motivation when they begin a project. The difficulty is keeping this driving force in mind when adversity appears. All too often people start a project but fail to complete it because they lose their motivation to do so. Take time to understand what motivates you and use it to push you across the finish line.

12) Take it easy

Sometimes emotional outbreaks occur because we don't take the time to slow down and process how we're feeling. Give yourself a break and make a conscious effort to meditate, do yoga or read – a little escapism works wonders. And then the next time you have an emotional reaction to something, try to pause before you react.

13) Acknowledge your emotional triggers

Self-aware individuals can recognize their emotions as they occur. It's important to be flexible with your emotions and adapt them to your situation. Don't deny your emotions at stage time but don't be rigid with them either, take the time to process your emotions before communicating them.

14) Predict how you will feel

Think about a situation you're going into and predict how you will feel. Practice naming and accepting the feelings – naming the feeling puts you in control. Try to choose an appropriate reaction to the feeling rather than just reacting to it.

15) Trust your intuition

If you are still unsure about which path to take, trust your intuition. After all, your subconscious has been learning which path to take throughout your entire life.

SELF MANAGEMENT

Once you've gotten to grips with self-awareness and how your emotions work, you can get a handle on self-management. This means taking responsibility for your behavior and well-being as well as controlling emotional outbursts.

16) Snap out of it

One key way to keep your emotions in check is to change your sensory input – motion dictates emotion as the old saying goes. So jolt your physical body out of routine by attending an exercise class or try channeling a busy mind with a puzzle or a book – anything to break your existing routine.

17) Maintain a schedule (and stick to it!)

Ensuring that you create a schedule and stick to it is extremely important if you want to complete tasks effectively.

"When you schedule appointments in your calendar, you're saying to yourself: "I'm going to do A, B and C by X date and it's going to take Y hours. Once you make this promise, it becomes harder to procrastinate."

18) Eat well

This sounds like an easy one but regulating what you eat and drink can have a massive effect on your emotional state, so try your best to maintain a balanced diet.

19) Don't get mad

Funnel your emotional energy into something productive. It's okay to keep overwhelming emotions inside, especially if it's not an appropriate time to let them out. However, when you do, rather than vent it on something futile, turn it into motivation instead. Don't get mad, get better.

20) Be interested

A key factor in managing yourself and your emotions is consciously taking the time to be interested in the subject matter, whether it be business or personal.

21) Don't expect people to trust you (if you can't trust them)

Establishing trust with a person can be difficult, and once it's lost it's very hard to regain. Try to be mindful that people are only human and will make mistakes. By offering your trust, you are inviting people to offer their trust in return.

22) It's your choice

You can choose how you react to a situation – you can either overreact or remain calm. But it's your choice.

MOTIVATION

A personal skills aspect of emotional intelligence, self-motivation refers to our inner drive to achieve and improve our commitment to our goals, our readiness to act on opportunities, and our overall optimism.

23) Personal goals

Personal goals can provide long-term direction and short-term motivation. So grab a pen and paper and think about where you want to be and set some targets for yourself. Base them on your strengths and make them relevant to you and ultimately, make them exciting and achievable. This task alone is enough to get you instantly motivated!

24) Be realistic

When you've set a new goal, be sure to give yourself realistic and clear aims to achieving that goal and understand that change is an inevitable part of life. Achievement boosts confidence and as self-confidence rises so does the ability to achieve more, see how it works.

25) Positive thinking

To keep motivated it's important to maintain an optimistic mindset. See problems and setbacks as learning opportunities instead of failings and try to avoid negative people and opt to surround yourself with positive, well-motivated people – they'll have a great effect on you.

26) Lifelong learning

Both knowledge and information are key for feeding your mind and keeping you curious and motivated. And with information so easily accessible, you have the opportunity to fuel your values and passions at the click of a button!

27) Be prepared to leave your comfort zone

The biggest barrier to achieving your full potential is not challenging yourself frequently enough. Great things can happen to you if you're willing to leave your comfort zone, so do so as often as you can.

28) Help

Don't be afraid to ask for help when you need it, and vice versa. If others need help, don't hold back in giving it to them. Seeing other people succeed will only help to motivate you.

29) Stand and stretch

For an instant short-term boost to your motivation, take a stand and stretch out as far as you can for 10 seconds. When you return to your desk, you'll be in the correct frame of mind and ready to work.

EMPATHY

Quite simply, empathy is the ability to understand other people's emotions. Understanding that everyone has their own set of feelings, desires, triggers, and fears. To be empathetic you're allowing their experiences to resonate with your own to respond in an emotionally appropriate way. It's a lifelong skill and the most important one for navigating relationships, and whilst it may not come naturally, there are a few ways it can be nurtured.

30) Listen

Before you're able to empathize with someone you first need to understand what it is they're saying, which means listening is at the very epicenter of empathy. It involves letting them talk without interruption, preconceptions, skepticism, and putting your issues on pause to allow yourself to absorb their situation and consider how they are feeling before you react.

31) Try to be approachable

Whether you're the leader of a team or working on a project with others, try to remain accessible and approachable.

32) Perspective

We're all familiar with the phrase "put yourself in their shoes", and this is exactly that. The simplest way of gaining a little perspective the next time an issue or situation arises is to switch places with the other person and think about what's happening from their point of view. Sometimes there's no right or wrong but at least you'll understand enough to come to resolve or offer some useful advice.

33) Open yourself up

One of the quickest ways to offer a sincere exchange or sign of empathy is to listen to someone's experiences and connect to them with a similar experience of your own. Don't be afraid to open yourself up, it might just be the start of a great and lasting friendship.

34) Immerse yourself in a new culture

The old saying 'travel broadens the mind' is still true, even in this ever-shrinking world. Sometimes the best way to open your mind is to jump on a plane and go somewhere completely different.

35) Cultivate curiosity about strangers

Highly empathetic people have an insatiable curiosity about strangers. When we talk to people outside of our usual social circle we learn about and begin to understand opinions, views, and lives that are different from our own. So next time you're sitting on a bus you know just what to do...

36) Acknowledge what people are saying

Another useful tip is, whilst listening to what a person has to say, use acknowledgment words such as 'I understand' and 'I see' to show a person you're listening (but of course only say these things if you are listening!).

SOCIAL SKILLS

In emotional intelligence terms, social skills refer to the skills needed to handle and influence other people's emotions effectively. It covers a wide range of abilities, from communication and conflict management to dealing with change, meeting new people, and building relationships, and plays a part in almost every part of our lives, from work life to our romantic life. It's complex and requires utilizing almost every point we have already mentioned, but here are a few pointers for you.

37) Get started

A good way to get started on improving your social skills is to isolate one skill you know you'd like to develop, this narrows it down and gives you focus. Internationally known psychologist, Daniel Goleman, suggests highlighting someone you know to be good at that particular skill, observing how they act and how they control their emotions, and then implementing and applying that knowledge to yourself.

38) Wear somebody else's shoes

Not literally of course! Everyone has heard the phrase 'walk a mile in somebody else's shoes, but how many people practice this advice? Give it a try, you never know.

39) Practice makes perfect

The idea of practicing your social skills might sound strange, but like everything in life, practice makes perfect.

40) Social media cold turkey

We don't mean to sound old, but taking your social life offline and engaging face-to-face with people will open up so many opportunities for you to gain and develop your social skills. So next time instead of instant messaging your best friend, meet up for a drink! Emotional intelligence doesn't expand within the confines of (un) social media...

41) Get networking

A good way to practice your social acumen is to attend local networking events. The great thing about these events is that everyone attending has a shared reason for attending.

42) It’s not what you say, it’s how you say it

We’re talking about the importance of nonverbal communication and how that can affect a person’s opinion of you. Body language, tone of voice, and eye contact are key to letting others know how you feel emotionally. So once you’ve got your emotions intact, think about how you’re physically coming across.

43) The unknown

The ultimate method to building your social skills is to get out there and be sociable. It sounds simple, but you can’t strengthen your social skills without being social! Join a group or network outside of your usual circle; it’s the perfect way to put all of our tips into play.

WHAT TO AVOID

Those with a high EQ very rarely display the following traits, something for you to be mindful of.

44) Drama

Emotionally intelligent people listen, offer sound advice, and extend empathy to those who need it but they don't permit others' lives and emotions to affect or rule their own.

45) Complaining

Complaining implies two things – one, that we are victims, and two, that there are no solutions to our problems. Rarely does an emotionally intelligent person feel victimized, and even more infrequently do they feel that a solution is beyond their grasp. So instead of looking for someone or something to blame, they think constructively and dissolve the solution in private.

46) Negativity

Emotionally intelligent people can curb cynical thoughts. They acknowledge that negative thoughts are just that – thoughts – and rely on facts to come to conclusions as well as being able to silence or zone out any negativity.

47) Dwelling on the past

Those with high emotional intelligence choose to learn from the mistakes and choices they have made and instead of dwelling on the past are mindful to live in the now.

48) Selfishness

Whilst a degree of selfishness is required to get ahead in life, too much can fracture relationships and cause disharmony. Try to avoid being overly selfish and consider other's needs.

49) Giving in to peer pressure

Just because everyone else does something, they don't feel compelled to follow suit if they don't want to. They think independently, and never conform just to please other people.

50) Being overly critical

Being too critical is the fastest way to lower someone's morale. Keep in mind that everyone is merely human and has the same desires (and restrictions) as you. Spend some time getting to know someone else before communicating the change you desire to see.

You too may realize your entire potential and accomplish your objectives by comprehending and effectively utilizing emotional intelligence.

www.ingramcontent.com/pod-product-compliance
Lightning Source LLC
LaVergne TN
LVHW050327160826
845677LV00014B/3558

* 9 7 9 8 3 5 2 7 8 1 7 0 8 *